From Whence We Came

College Survival Toolkit

"Pick It Up, and Take Out What You Need"

Compiled by LEAP Forward, Inc.
and
Concerned Black Women of Calvert County

Submissions from Past and Present College Students

ISBN 978-0-692-90956-0

Printed by RS Graphx, Inc.

Design and Layout by Rhonda Rawlings-Saunders, RS Graphx, Inc.
Editorial Services by Darlene Harrod
One Line Art by Sir Shadow, New York, New York
Poetry by Nathaniel D. Clayton, Philadelphia, PA
Messages by Student Contributors

Dedication and Introduction

The *From Whence We Came College Survival Toolkit* is dedicated to all students in various educational pursuits. This resource aims to provide wisdom and real-world experiences to students seeking college degrees. Included are statements from 31 current and former college students to help you with your transition into college life. Twenty-nine are past scholarship recipients. All completed their high school education in Maryland or Washington D.C. What better voices to hear from than those who have traveled the journey you are about to embark on. They know the joys and the struggles, and they want you to become aware.

Rhonda Thomas, President of LEAP Forward Inc., and Nicole Cooksey, President of Concerned Black Women of Calvert County, "old-school" college graduates, whose reflections are also included, realized a need for the book after numerous conversations with students, parents, teachers, and other community activists and leaders over the years. With love, concern, and those conversations in mind, the presidents collaborated to fill the need. Read more about their organizations on pages 47 through 53.

You are not expected to read this book from cover to cover. It is a toolkit! Please pull from it when you need guidance and encouragement. Some of the specific message areas shared include the following: Embrace the Ivy League Experience, Transferring May Enter Your Thoughts, Use Study Groups, Prepare for Homesickness, Do Not Abuse Your Unsupervised Freedom, Always Be Yourself, Keep God First, Friendships Will Gravitate to You, Where There Is a Will, There Will Be a Way to Pay for Your Education, Practice Good Work Ethics, Have No Fear, and Do Not Doubt.

The messages reflect honest encounters experienced by our contributors. Without their desire to share, this toolkit would not be possible and this knowledge would not be passed on to you. Thank you contributors. The list of message areas can be found on page 1.

From Whence We Came is intended for students in all walks of their "educational careers." Whether you choose a 2-year trade school or a 4-year college or university, pursuing your degree will become your "job" after high school. You are now a "career student," and your job becomes getting an education. The advice and principles offered can be applied no matter what form of higher education you are seeking.

Prayerfully, you will find the students' wisdom and experiences useful.

Pick It Up, and Take Out What You Need. – Make It Your Toolkit.

Student Contributors

Tyler Austin
Joseph Berry
Jessica Brooks
Michelle Brooks
Keshia Capers
Caira Cartwright
Jadea Deahl
Randl Dent
Andrew Dupree
Phillip Dupree

Kelsey Edwards
Kendra Edwards
Cedric Fowler
Shalonda Holt
Jai Horsey
Trayonna Hutchins
Kyle Hutzler
Kevin Jackson, Jr.
Autumn James
Jerrell Jones
Samantha Jones

Pierce Jordan
Matthew Lewis
Symphony Love
Riddicia Mackall
Beth Mead
Brandon Perkins
Aleia Plenty
Wilbur Robinson
Shala Thomas
Tiffany Toye

Since 2017, some of our Student Contributors have graduated college, started careers and businesses, and are engaged in other exciting adventures such as graduate school or law school. The advice they shared in 2017 is still pertinent and produced great results. We are proud of every one of them.

2021 Update on Our Student Contributors

Tyler Austin
Accountant at TMJA, LLC

Joseph Berry
IT Professional

Jessica Brooks
Entrepreneur

Michelle Brooks
Federal Government Contracting Officer

Keshia Capers
Chemical Engineer with the Navy

Caira Cartwright
Operations Supervisor at Maryland Department of Human Services

Jadea Deahl
Legal Assistant at Sawyer & Myerberg

Randi Dent
Health Equity Scholar at George Washington University

Andrew Dupree
Product Manager at Dexterity Inc.

Phillip Dupree
Mechanical Engineer at Lyft

Kelsey Edwards
Obstetrics & Gynecology Physician Assistant at NYU Langone Health

Kendra Edwards
Program Coordinator for The Center for Life Enrichment/LMU Duncan School of Law – pursuing Law Degree

Cedric Fowler
Automotive Professional

Shalonda Holt
2016 Washington Post Teacher of the Year (Biology)

Jai Horsey
Graduate student at Indiana University of Medicine

Trayonna Hutchins
2020 UMCP Cum Laude Graduate with Bachelor of Arts in Theater

Kyle Hutzler
Senior Associate at McKinsey & Company

Kevin Jackson, Jr.
Master's in Electrical Engineer completed works for the Navy

Autumn James
Second Year J.D. candidate at the University of Baltimore School of Law

Jerrell Jones
Mechanical Engineer at Ford Motor Company

2021 Update on Our Student Contributors

Samantha Jones
Technology Consulting
Manager at Accenture

Matthew (Isaiah) Lewis
Bachelor's Degree in
Communications Studies
with Concentration in
Leadership

Riddicia Mackall
Certified Public Accountant

Beth Mead
Computer Scientist for the
Navy

Brandon Perkins
Associate's Degree in
Computer Technology
with Concentration in
Cybersecurity
from Allegany College of
Maryland

Aleia Plenty
Law Clerk at SMGQ Law
(Third Year Law Student at
University of Miami)

Wilbur Robinson
Cyber Security Major at
University of Maryland
Global Campus

Shala Thomas
Content Producer at KJRH-
TV NBC Channel 2 News in
Tulsa

Tiffany Toye
Presales Consultant at
Cigna

Table of Discussions

Tyler
Austin

Patuxent High School, 2011
Salisbury University

Key Points

1. Be Yourself
2. Friendships Will Gravitate to You

Your first year of college is very important. The difficulty of your classes will be much less than those in the following years, but many students dig themselves into a hole by not taking it seriously. Your first year is perfect to put yourself ahead by getting a high GPA. This will help you when you get to the more difficult courses later and allow you the chance to recover if you don't do so well in a class. Try to also take more credits and classes than the minimum. You don't want to get to your last year and have a bunch of classes to still take in order to graduate.

Now, as far as meeting new people and making new friends, don't worry too much. Just be yourself and don't worry about impressing anyone. A lot of students make the mistake of trying to become a new person in order to get others' approval and friendships. Those who are meant for you will gravitate to you and if it is not many, well, a few great friends are better than a bunch of fake friends.

Have faith, and follow your heart.

Joseph
Berry

Calvert High School, 2015
Coastal Carolina University, Sophomore

Key Points

1. Practice Time Management
2. Establish Priorities
3. Set Goals

My years at college have taught me that I have to be able to manage my time and take care of my priorities. There will be times when you will be distracted by other things (school events, parties, friends, procrastination), but you have to be able to put your priorities in order.

I have also learned that you have to surround yourself with people who have the same or bigger goals than you have. Being around likeminded people will help you achieve your goals. If you surround yourself with people who don't have the same goals or no goals at all, you will find yourself straying away from what you need to do.

Jessica
Brooks

Calvert High School, 2004
Morgan State University, 2008

Key Points

1. Demonstrate Ingenuity and Perseverance
2. Stay in Your Lane
3. Focus
4. Use Discernment in Taking Advice
5. Face Challenges

Being an unconventional person, attending college allowed me to demonstrate ingenuity and perseverance regardless of the challenge. And yes, there will be challenges that you will face. If you fail a class, it's not the end of the world. Don't get along with roommates? Well, you cannot be everyone's friend. Stay in your lane, and focus on your education so that you can be competitive in this world.

Professors and advisors will have their own ideas of what they feel will help you in life. You must use discernment and gage what will be helpful and what will hinder your future. You have more opportunities awaiting you that were not available to me. Take advantage, and do something different to become a well-rounded person.

Michelle
Brooks

Calvert High School, 2006
Bowie State University, 2010

Key Points

1. Handholding Not Allowed
2. Grow Up or Go Home

I couldn't afford college, but my mother encouraged me to attend anyway. Every semester I questioned how I would pay for the next. It wasn't until the last semester of my senior year that I was able to purchase all of my textbooks. But through it all, I graduated magna cum laude.

In college, I learned handholding was not allowed. Students had two options: Grow up. Or go home. I chose to grow up.
I learned to face obstacles with a "so-what" attitude and a "will-do" determination. And that persistence helped me through college and into the working world.

If you feel unprepared for your college journey, remember each experience will prepare you for the next step. I pray that God will be with you on this adventure, and I know your testimony will inspire the next Freshman Class.

Keshia
Capers

Calvert High School, 2013
Hampton University

Key Points

1. Participate in Pre-College Activities
2. ASK
3. Embrace Networking
4. Better Yourself

Going off to college was the best decision I have made. I am majoring in Chemical Engineering at Hampton University. As the first in my immediate family to go off to college, this is a big deal for me! I attended Hampton's Pre-College and Summer Bridge Program, a 5-week, academic enrichment, residential program the summer before my freshman year. It was an awesome experience. Being in this program gave me first-hand knowledge of how campus life works and the opportunity to learn my way around campus before the whole campus was filled to capacity with students.

Some advice I would give to future college students is not to be afraid to ask for help. No matter what you need help in— life, school, friendships, or anything, just ask. Sometimes, you will need to put your pride aside and get the assistance you need. Another word of advice is to network. Always try to make a good impression so any person you meet will always remember you. I have attended many career fairs and waited until the spring semester of my sophomore year to network with the many people I had met. Through networking, you make connections and meet people who can help you in many ways with internships, letters of recommendation, and many other things. College is a great experience full of great memories, making lifetime friendships, and overall bettering yourself.

Caira
Cartwright

St. Mary's College, 2014

Key Points

1. Improve Your Life
2. Catapult Your Life
3. Commute to College
4. Join Support Groups

I smile when I think back on my first college experiences. Though it felt like a whirlwind of essays, deadlines, and late nights, I am happy with how a college degree has improved my life. It does seem that the purpose of college is just that—designed to catapult your life into something bigger, brighter, and faster. I went through all 4 years of college as a commuter student, staying home with my family, while driving to classes each day. Even though where I slept didn't change, the college experience changed my life. I appreciate my college career—from the professors I had discussions and worked with—to the friends I slept over with, studied with, and who encouraged my development and success. I am so thankful and proud that I had the opportunity to get my bachelor's degree. I hope to give back to my community in the way that LEAP Forward has! Completing college with a support group makes all the difference!

Jadea
Deahl

Patuxent High School, 2015
Towson University

I am a sophomore pursuing my undergraduate degree. My advice is going to focus on what to do in high school and in those first couple of years in college.

First, challenge yourself in high school. I know that once you get to be a junior and senior, getting to college is so close, but so far away, to the point where you are just ready for high school to be done. But this is when you really must step it up into high gear and continue to do the absolute best you can. A lot of people think that once you are admitted into a college, that you are good to go, but this is not always the case. Many colleges will require your final transcript, which means your grades will matter all the way to the very end! In other words, keep your grades up in high school. You never really understand how important having a good GPA is until you are applying for schools and scholarships, and trust me, those scholarships are so helpful.

Second, along with wanting high school to be over as quickly as possible, don't forget to have fun. I could not STAND it when people told me, "Enjoy high school because before you know it, it'll be over." I just mocked them, thinking no way. I cannot wait until college. But I quickly came to realize that when you do go to college, you're an adult, and "adulting" is not always peaches and cream. The reality is, college work is a lot harder and more time consuming than in high school, and those 4 years of school really will fly by. So, when you hear this from people reminiscing about their childhood, just remember to take advantage of the fact that you still have time to actually enjoy your high school and college years.

In your first couple of weeks of college, just try everything out. That means, don't be so hasty to move out of your community-style dorm; don't automatically not go to the dining hall just because you heard it wasn't good; and above all, don't be opposed to meeting new people. While these things may suck, everyone is going through the suck together. The best way to get through it is to make friends with those people who also think it sucks, and talk about how bad it sucks together. In all seriousness, some of my best friends have come out of those first couple of weeks. Read your book assignments on time. Let me tell you, professors will give you a syllabus at the beginning of the semester and will not mention any of the assigned readings after that. You will think this is liberating, until you get that first quiz or exam and it's ALL based on the reading that YOU didn't do. Taking good notes during lectures is important, but I suggest keeping up on the assigned readings.

Next, don't be afraid to go to your professors' office hours; they are there for a reason. Many good things can come out of it: checking up on your grades before the semester is over, getting help on your homework, or even getting little hints about a quiz or exam. Going to your professors also can help you gain a relationship with them that will show them that you care which can benefit you in the long run.

Third, join some clubs. Getting involved is not just something that looks good on a job resume (which it does), but it's also something that helps you to get out and meet new people. There are many people from various places who you can meet. So why not? Being involved also keeps you busy, which forces you to prioritize. I'm not saying I never procrastinate, but being involved in sports and clubs helped me to not wait until the night before a due date to write a paper because I knew I would have to wake up for practice or have a meeting the next day.

Fourth, get out and explore your college town. No matter where you go, a big school or a small school, there is going to be something unique about the area you are in. This way you are not shutting yourself in your dorm just doing homework. Getting out gives you that special connection to your school and helps you to cope with the "more challenging things" like grades, midterms, and papers.

Last, but not least, say Thank You to the people who have helped you along the way. Whether it's a mom, dad, grandparent, teacher, or friend, they all want to see you succeed and do well in whatever it is you want to do. Just make sure to let them know how grateful you are for their support.

These are just some of the things that I hope to continue to do, or do better. I'm still young and still have some learning and growing to do myself, but I hope that I could help you to at least get started planning for college.

Cheers and good luck!

Randl
Dent

Northern High School, 2011
Washington and Lee University, 2015
Virginia Commonwealth University, 2018

Key Points

1. Embrace Networking
2. Allow Others to Challenge Your Viewpoints
3. Stand Up for What You Believe and Yourself

I am currently a second-year doctoral student in the Health Psychology program at Virginia Commonwealth University (VCU). I graduated in 2011 from Northern High School located in Owings, Maryland. For my undergraduate degree, I attended Washington and Lee University (W&L) located in Lexington, Virginia. At W&L, I majored in psychology and sociology. After I graduated in May 2015 with a Bachelor of Arts Degree in Psychology, I moved to Richmond, Virginia, where I currently reside. In addition to my classes at VCU, I also work as an undergraduate advisor for psychology majors. I have the pleasure of empowering students to take ownership of their college experience and guiding them in the achievement of their personal and academic goals.

My advice for students: College is not only a time for education, but also for self-exploration and growth. I encourage you to meet new people, experience new things, and venture out of your comfort zone! In addition, I encourage you to network with both your fellow students and your professors. My faculty advisor at W&L was invaluable in my search to figure out whether graduate school was for me. I have been out of undergraduate college for almost 2 years, and I still keep in contact with my professors and meet up with them when I visit W&L. Lastly, I encourage you to stand up for what you believe in, and also allow others to challenge your viewpoints. I've learned and grown immensely, not only from the situations during which I decided to stand up for myself (and others like me), but also from the situations in which others challenged my beliefs.

Andrew
Dupree

University of Maryland, 2011
Stanford, 2014

Key Points

1. Be Responsible
2. Do Not Drown in Unsupervised Freedom
3. Develop Self-discipline

College is a unique experience. Never again will you be on your own, surrounded by thousands of new peers, with an ocean of potential life trajectories at your fingertips. It is a huge opportunity—but what is often overlooked is how much *responsibility* it is as well.

At the University of Maryland, I spent 3 years working in the dormitory for the Honors program as a Resident Assistant. My job was to help my students have a positive experience in dorm life and a good year of college. I observed about 150 of the school's brightest new students start their college career. Most of them had an exciting and fulfilling college experience—but a trivial amount never returned for their second or third year of school. These students seemed to be having a good time in the dorms—making friends, having fun, going out on the weekends. But I would later learn they were skipping classes, sleeping or playing video games most of the day, not studying or doing their homework, etc. In brief, they drowned in the unsupervised freedom of the college experience.

The hardest part of the college experience won't be your coursework. It will be keeping yourself on task, staying focused, and being responsible every day for 4 (or more!) years. It's a daunting task, but if you can develop this required self-discipline, it will help you achieve everything you want for the rest of your life.

Good luck to you.

Phillip **Dupree**

Columbia University, 2011

Key Points

1. Find Your Niche
2. Find Your Community— Friends

I left home for Columbia University in New York City in the fall of 2007. And oh, how little I knew. The transition from the quiet suburbs of Maryland to the Upper West Side of Manhattan was an interesting one. I remember being afraid to ride the subway by myself, sure I would get lost somewhere in the wilds of New York City. Furthermore, I was surrounded by peers from every corner of the world. Though there were friends to make and amazing conversations to be had, the competition was intense, and the workload was brutal. I had a lot to learn.

My advice is twofold. One, do everything you can to find your niche and your community. College takes a lot out of you. You're working long hours (or at least you should be!). You're constantly being challenged by your peers, your professors, and the new environment you're adjusting to. You're pouring yourself out constantly, and unless you find others to pour into you, you'll find yourself empty before long. So take risks. If you see a group playing basketball or Frisbee, don't be afraid to ask to join in. Strike up a conversation with the person next to you in the cafeteria line. Especially during the first few weeks of school, everyone is trying to make friends. Organizations are one of the easiest ways to meet people, and you will have a baseline of something in common. Whether a religious group, a volunteer organization, an academic club, or an athletic activity, student groups are one of the best and easiest ways to meet your peers, and find your place.

And two, don't be afraid if it takes time to find that community. In my first year at the university, I fell into a group of friends who were not bad people, but they weren't great friends either. In retrospect, I can see they tore me down more than they built me up. Though I did make some good friends and memories during my first 2 years of college, I didn't really find my stride until my junior year. I found new friends and activities I loved by becoming a Resident Advisor and mentoring a high school robotics team run out of my university. More adventures than I can count followed from these connections, and my last 2 years of school were far better than the first two. So don't give up if things do not fall into place immediately.

Good luck and Godspeed!

Kelsey
Edwards

Patuxent High School, 2009
Lincoln Memorial University, 2013
DeBusk College of Osteopathic Medicine,
    Physician Assistant Program 2018

Key Points

1. Remember Your Goals
2. Form a Support System of God, Parents, Family, Teachers, and Friends
3. Read Jeremiah 29:11
4. Do Your Best to Be the Best
5. Step Out of Your Comfort Zone

In preparing for the freshman year of college, there are all types of things that will soon be going through your head. How am I going to make it through my first year? How am I going to make it without my parents? Am I going to make any friends? How will I juggle schoolwork and a social life? These are all questions similar to what I asked myself 8 years ago during the summer before my freshman year. It was overwhelming to say the least. But the most helpful thing to ease my mind was talking to students who had already walked through the journey I was about to embark on. Their advice and transparency in sharing experiences helped me through my undergraduate years. So here is the advice I pass on to you as you prepare to take on what you will one day call the BEST years of your life.

Remember your goals: You have the ability to do anything you want to do. Never let anyone tell you differently. Use the support system of God, your parents, family, or whomever you lean on when you find yourself struggling. Along with my parents, I referred to Jeremiah 29:11 when the going got tough. It reads, "For I know the plans I have for you, declares the Lord, plans to prosper you and not to harm you, plans to give you hope and a future." On graduation day, I decided to place that verse on my graduation cap as a symbol of my journey. There will be many times when you want to stand on your own, but as my teacher once said, "If you want to go quickly through life, go alone…. If you want to go far in life, go together." Teachers, family, and friends are all there to help you.

Many of us try to "find ourselves" in college, but what many don't realize is that in order to find yourself, you have to get a little lost first. So don't be afraid to step out of your comfort zone. Join clubs, meet new people, have fun, but always remember your main goals. As Dr. Seuss once said, "Life's a balancing act." Balance the fun with the studies. Don't do something today that will hinder you tomorrow.

Do what you have to do today so you can do what you WANT to do tomorrow. You'll have plenty of days where you would rather go hang out with friends instead of studying for an exam, or instead of going to work. But when you get done what you have to do, being able to do what you WANT to do is a lot closer than you think.

Lastly, Abraham Lincoln once said, "Whatever you are, be a good one." Whether you graduate and go to college, or if you graduate and go straight into the workforce, it is important to remember to do your best in order to be your best. Of course, you'll laugh. You'll cry. You'll have good days. You'll have days that are a train wreck. You'll make good friends. You'll make LIFETIME friends. But whatever you do, do it well.

Kelsey

Kendra
Edwards

Patuxent High School, 2007
California University of Pennsylvania, 2011

Key Points

1. Student Athletes Must Live Up to a High Standard
2. Athletes Must Have a Passion for Sports
3. Study What Is Interesting to You
4. Have an End Goal in Sight

College was quite a bit of an interesting time for me. I played Varsity soccer for 4 years while at Patuxent High School. I went on to play at High Point University Division I level, and that is where it became a little stressful for me. For many people, being away from home for the first time can be quite overwhelming. I would honestly say that if you do play a sport and plan to do so in college, and even for a team after college, make sure that you have a passion for it. Student athletes have a high standard to live up to—going to class, going to practice (sometimes two or three times a day), attending study hall, and adjusting to college life. It can be quite overbearing for many people. Do not get me wrong; this is a personal opinion. I would most definitely play soccer in college again, just not on the Division I level.

Aside from that, I went into college with a very good understanding of what I wanted to study, and that is most important. I stumbled upon two criminal justice classes while attending Patuxent High School and was hooked from there. I knew that if it pertained to law or the criminal justice system, it was something that I immediately took interest in. I took as many criminal justice courses in college as I could. On two occasions, I was given the opportunity to visit maximum-security prisons and speak with inmates who had been accused of many different things. My advice would be to stick with a course of study that you find interesting, and one that you could see yourself working in once you graduate from college.

The biggest thing with succeeding in college was to stay focused and to connect with positive people on a mission to do extremely well and excel in everything they set their minds to. College should be the most exciting experience and a place to meet new people, make new friends, and learn about the cultures and backgrounds of everyone around you. Everyone has a different story.

I graduated from California University in 2011 with a Bachelor's Degree in Criminal Justice and a minor in Corporate and Homeland Security. I then went on to get a Master's Degree in Law and Public Policy, and I am currently working for a law firm in Washington, D.C. I am now in the process of applying to law school to continue my dream of becoming an attorney.

My words of wisdom: College will present many challenges and hardships. You will encounter and see things that you are not used to. Please, please, please, remember that you have an end goal in sight and stay focused on that, even though things may seem like they are not going well. Once you complete what you have set out to do, whether it be receiving just a bachelor's, or going on to get your master's, no one can take that away from you!

I am always open to speaking with anyone about college. My email address is edw8365@gmail.com!

Kendra

Cedric
Fowler

Calvert High School, 2016
Morgan State University

Key Points

1. Find Balance
2. Make Wise Choices
3. Make Good Decisions about Spending Money
4. Practice Time Management

College is a big change from high school. The classes get harder and other responsibilities are present outside of the classroom. You must do your own laundry, and wake yourself up for class in the morning. My experience in college my first semester was a good one and it helped me gage how ready I really am for the next 4 years. I could wake up and go to my morning classes, and I could find a good balance between school and my social life. Sometimes, it was difficult to choose between going out with friends or staying inside and studying.

One thing I learned about being in college is how important it really is to save money. When I first got to Morgan, I spent a lot of money and did not realize how much I was spending until it was almost gone. But towards the end of the semester, I started to make good decisions about spending money. In conclusion, the leap from high school to college is big, and you have to be ready to tackle the next stage of your education.

Shalonda
Holt

Calvert High School, 2002
University of Maryland Baltimore County, 2007
McDaniel, 2012

Key Points

1. Follow Your Passion
2. Never Give Up
3. GPS—Gift, Purpose, and Strengths

My advice for students who are preparing for college is to follow YOUR passion. I knew I had a passion for biology, but I felt that everyone wanted me to become a doctor. I quickly realized that was not my dream, but that teaching was. I did not have to BECOME a teacher; it was who I was. It was ingrained in me. It was in my DNA. As my grandmother would always tell me, "You want to find a career that you want not one that you are forced to have."

It is also important to stay the course; never give up. As Maya Angelou said, "You may encounter many defeats, but you must not be defeated." Life is a journey. There are many paths and many routes you can take to reach your final destination. There may be unforeseen bumps in the road along the way, but just remember to use your GPS—your Gift, Purpose, and Strengths as you navigate through life.

Shalonda Holt was named The *Washington Post's* 2016 Teacher of the Year, formerly known as the Agnes Meyer Outstanding Teacher Award.

Jai
Horsey

Northern High School, 2015
Morgan State University

Key Points

1. Keep God First
2. Practice Time Management
3. Watch Your Free Time

I attend Morgan State University in Baltimore, Maryland, where I study Biology in the Honors program. I am currently a sophomore with a cumulative 3.4 GPA, while also maintaining leadership roles in the President's Leadership Circle, the Morgan M.I.L.E. (Male Initiative on Leadership and Excellence), and a work-study job at the Alumni House. I also have been affiliated with the Student Government Association and made the Dean's List.

My accomplishments at Morgan are extremely sacred to me, and although I remain humble, I state them proudly. There are two main reasons why I am successful in college: God and time management. God has always been my Father, my provider, and literally **my everything**. Without Him in my life, I would be nothing, and my life would be empty. As far as time management, these words are constantly said when people address the most important features of college and even life. Prior to attending college, I heard the words numerous times, but I never truly understood the meaning. Although they sounded straightforward, the words were actually a much more complex concept. But, what is time management really? I have learned that time management is the balance between what you **want** to do and what you **have** to do.

In college, free time is the downfall of many students, but also the catalyst to success. Free time is when you can party and go out, but it is also the time when you can study or get extra help. Free time can be used to sleep, or it can be used to read. The truth is neither extreme by itself is healthy. Personally speaking, I have had moments when I have been at both extremes. I can say from experience that a strictly social life in college clearly corrupts your academics and vice versa. My accomplishments are a result of me finding my balance between my social life and academics. I do believe that everyone has their own specific variation of balance, but success comes when you find ways to achieve your goals and have time to have fun too.

Trayonna **Hutchins**

Huntingtown High School, 2016
University of Maryland College Park, Freshman

Key Points

1. Have No Fear
2. Seek Help
3. Practice Good Work Ethics
4. Your Health Comes First

The first semester of my college education has provided me with perhaps the most difficult yet most rewarding moments of my life. From day one, I have encountered a plethora of brand new experiences: living with a roommate, my first job, college classes, using public transportation, dealing with all the things that come with growing up, etc. I have been challenged in ways that I've never had to endure. I quickly discovered that the college tales about sleepless nights, tears, and junk food were becoming truer than I had hoped. And yet, I was blessed enough to be able to walk away with straight A's and a leading role in the upcoming Spring Semester's theatrical production of The *Amish Project*.

If I could pass on two pieces of advice I would say that one, don't be afraid to seek help. And I don't mean procrastinating on a project and then asking a teacher for more time. Take initiative, and take full advantage of the opportunities presented to you. I would not have received half the success I have today if it were not for the kindness and the generosity of the people around me willing to help. Sign up for scholarships, and do it early! Have your teachers or a peer proofread your essays. Take a tour of the colleges that you're interested in and make connections. Visit a teacher during office hours and ask for advice. Ask an upperclassman about college life or classes. So many people want to see you succeed. All you have to do is ask.

Two, now is the most important time for you to put your best foot forward.

I received a full ride for the first semester of college, and as I previously stated; I obtained straight A's; I worked a part time job while taking 16 credits; and I was a part of two theatre productions. Now I may not be the smartest person, nor am I the most talented, but I am blessed to have good work ethics. You can't afford to stay idle. By consistently working hard, many good things will come your way. There will be times in college when you will doubt that you can do any more. There is always going to be someone a little bit smarter or a little more prepared. In those moments, remember to never rest on your intelligence. Hard work beats brains, hands down, every time! That being said, work hard, but take on only what you can handle. Don't overwhelm yourself. Your health comes first, and that means getting enough to eat and sleep. It's easy to forget that sometimes while juggling the group projects, club activities, auditions, and final assignments. Do what you love, and do it to the best of your personal ability.

Kyle
Hutzler

Huntingtown High School, 2010
Yale, 2014
Schwarzman Scholar, 2017
Stanford, 2019

1. Have an Open Mind
2. Embrace the Ivy League Experience
3. Read, Conference, Write
4. Be Willing to Learn
5. Study a Foreign Language
6. Get Mentors
7. Do Not Doubt
8. Find a Core Group of Friends

Anywhere I went with an open mind and a willingness to learn at Yale, I gained something from the experience. Whether it was conversations that started at breakfast and kept going straight through lunch, late nights in common rooms, simply walking the streets of New Haven, quiet moments of reflection at the Art Gallery, or a day spent wandering the stacks in our library, I learned things about the world and myself in those 4 years that I am still only beginning to appreciate.

I am a big believer in the Francis Bacon quotation that "Reading makes a full man; conference a ready man; and writing an exact man." In other words, read as much as you can, talk and listen as much as you can, and write as much as you can. (Ample sleep and eating healthy don't hurt either.)

You owe it to yourself to study a foreign language. Studying Spanish and Chinese have opened opportunities to me that have changed my life. Much of our future will be driven by technology and data; so, no matter what your major, I believe everyone should take a coding, statistics, or a data science class.

It might take a while to find them, but once you have gotten a core group of friends in your life who inspire you to be a better person in some way, don't let them go. Mentors can make an incredible difference. You have to put yourself out there to find them. Go to office hours just to talk. And sometimes, the best mentors are those just a few years older than you who can help you "see around the corner" and help you be better prepared.

Lastly, even on the toughest days, don't ever doubt that you deserve to be at wherever you have chosen to go to school. There are people—including those you have never met—rooting for and are proud of you.

Schwarzman Scholars is a new yearlong master's program on U.S.-China relations.

Kevin
Jackson, Jr.

Patuxent High School, 2014
College of Southern Maryland

Key Points

1. Make Connections
2. Get Involved
3. Use Study Groups

I am a sophomore pursuing a degree in Electrical Engineering at the College of Southern Maryland. My advice and wisdom to a college student would be to make connections, get involved, and find your niche. Joining clubs, societies, fraternities, etc., are great ways to make connections and friends. These connections and friends can help you get internships, jobs, etc. I have received multiple internship opportunities simply because of the connections that I made with different people from clubs and organizations. College is a place with many opportunities. Take advantage of them as much as possible.

My next word of advice would be to integrate study groups into your college experience. Find a strong and reliable study group that you can study with and hang out with every once in a while. It is important because classes can get hard and working together is a good way to stay focused and get things done. In addition, college can be difficult, but by working together you can help each other overcome the feeling of being lost, always have someone to check over your work, succeed in the classroom, make friends, and much more.

Autumn
James' Insight

Huntingtown High School, 2015

Key Points

1. Look at Colleges Early
2. Learn to Co-exist
3. Be Ready–Get Ready
4. Seize the Moment
5. Work Comes First

As I prepared for college, I often found myself to be frazzled. My grandmother was the only person in my immediate family who received a higher education. With that being so long ago, my family often struggled to help me apply and prepare for college. I remember applying to literally 20 schools simply because I did not have a clue of where I wanted to go. I would advise high school students to start looking at schools no later than the beginning of your junior year so it does not hit you all at once. I would also advise students to prepare for academic and social adjustments.

Before going to Spelman College, I was very shy, and for the most part, I stayed to myself. I realized on move in day that this could not be the case for me in college. For the first time in my life, I had a roommate, and I would have to, at the very least, co-exist with someone else in a small space. Luckily, for me, she is one of my closest friends now. My roommate was able to reassure me and remind me that all of us were struggling with similar things. After finishing my first semester, I realized that I would be okay, and I was no longer overwhelmed. Of course, everyone will have tough days or even weeks, but that is completely normal. All of the stress and hard work I put into getting to this moment were well worth it. My family and high school prepared me well for the workload of college by keeping me busy with sports, clubs, and schoolwork. I would also advise anyone preparing for college to be ready for an abundance of assignments, exams, and essays.

Although I am only a sophomore, I can already tell that these 4 years are going to fly by. I often hear people say, "College is the best 4 years of your life." Every time someone says this I am taken aback, and I have to remember to seize the moment. You have to make the best of each and every second. While I strongly suggest being involved in clubs and socializing with friends on campus, it is most important to remember that your work comes first. College is an adjustment solely because you no longer have anyone to make sure you wake up for class or to put you in check when you want to go out with your friends but know you have a test at 9 o'clock the next morning. The moment you stay in your room to prepare for an exam or take a trip to the library to study instead of going out is when you become a responsible student. Your future is in your hands!

Jerrell Jones

Northern High School, 2016
North Carolina Agricultural & Technical State University,
Freshman

Key Points

1. Find Like-minded Friends

2. Prepare Daily and Weekly Agendas

3. Sit in the Front of the Class

4. Use Stress Relievers

College is an experience in which you grow as a person and learn. It is important to first surround yourself with a good core group of friends who have the same aspirations and goals as you have. After you establish your main friends, it is imperative to network and introduce yourself to a great majority of people because you never know when they might be able to help you somewhere down the road. Never forget where you came from and where you plan to go. School comes first, and everything else falls in afterwards.

For me, it was beneficial to write out a daily and weekly agenda so that I could stay on top of tasks. When in class, sit in the front so that the professor can become familiar with your face or even your name. If you are unclear about anything discussed in class, do not hesitate to go to that professor during office hours because sometimes they do a better job explaining in their office than in class. Form study groups for classes so that you can bounce ideas off someone else and comprehend the material. It is also very important to find something that can relieve you of stress. For me, it is going to the gym. Have fun as you experience your first little taste of the real world.

Samantha **Jones**

Northern High School, 2010
University of Pennsylvania Bachelor of Science Degree, 2014
Master of Science Degree, 2015

Key Points

1. Welcome to the College Environment
2. Take Your First Semester's Performance Seriously
3. There are Other "Smart Kids" on Campus
4. Acknowledge the Importance of Good Study Habits
5. Realize that College is Not High School
6. Consider the Possibility of Getting Your First Bad Grade

My first year in college was a learning experience and a reality check. I was prepared for college to be challenging, and I was prepared to work hard and take interesting courses. However, I do not think I fully understood the environment that I would be entering. Throughout my elementary, middle, and high school years, I was used to doing well, and I expected that to continue. School subjects and concepts generally came easily to me, and I could expect to do well on exams with a quick cram session the night or morning before an exam in my car in the school parking lot. When I chose my classes for my first semester at the University of Pennsylvania (PENN), I was prepared for several "repeats" and to simply bolster the knowledge that I had already gained in subjects I was familiar with. However, despite planning a first semester I thought I was well prepared for, I didn't do well.

I was not used to not doing well. And I questioned my intelligence, my acceptance to PENN, my major, and everyone who had told me throughout my life that I was a "smart kid." I struggled that semester, and nothing "came easy" to me in the semesters that followed. I realized that I came to college thinking that things would continue to come easily, that I was fully prepared, and that I wouldn't necessarily need to fight for my spot at the "top" that I was so used to holding. And while I had the "tools" I needed to succeed, I had never really been required to use them. I learned that I really had never studied for anything in my life, and I wasn't used to asking for help or extra practice.

So my advice for new and current college students would be to not ever question your intelligence or your place at your university. But don't be afraid or too proud to ask for help, to go to tutoring, to join study groups, to go to study halls, etc. Even if you have never needed to use those tactics before to succeed, college is an entirely new environment full of "smart kids." A place will challenge you and force you out of your comfort zone. Be prepared to seek help and take ownership of your education and your experience. And once you become comfortable in that setting, don't settle. Don't become satisfied with "good enough" or "passing." Be determined to continue to be a learner who thrives.

Pierce
Jordan

Huntingtown High School, 2011
Temple University

Key Points

1. Value Hard Work
2. Build Self-worth
3. Develop Tools and Good Habits
4. Focus and Become Aware

I was a 2011 recipient of a LEAP Forward Scholarship at Huntingtown High School in Huntingtown, Maryland. I'm now 8 months removed from completing my undergraduate studies at Temple. Some of the most important things that I have and still am learning are concepts, not situational adages stored as an unused mental compilation. I have learned the value of hard work, and how that value comes from within. Knowing your worth allows you to know which is the best foot to first put forward, and to be able to accept nothing less than what your work deserves because you are fully aware of how thorough and well-done it is. This sense of self-worth builds confidence and patience. Confidence comes from the assuredness of a job well-done. Patience is born of that knowledge of self and worth, allowing you to give yourself the time you need to do your best work.

I have learned these things from my partial detachment to my college career. I wasn't interested in having the standard college experience, or any, to be honest. I was only interested in music, and I knew that I had to get my degree before I could more fully commit myself to creation on the terms that I knew I needed to. I want to create art that informs my experiences in life, and takes me around the world to new knowledge, feelings, and people who share a commonality of the two with me. I say this to say that I learned at Temple that for some people college isn't about coming to a decision based on the tools you've been given because of an enormous decision you, as an 18 or 19 year old, were forced to make prematurely. For me, instead, college was a place where I began to develop the tools and habits that I need to continue on a path of achievement in the area of my life that I could never divert my attention from for anything. I became more focused the more I became aware of what I really wanted to be doing.

Matthew
Lewis

Annapolis High School, 2016
Frostburg State University

Key Points

1. Schedule Study Time
2. Set Sleep Time
3. Prepare for Homesickness
4. Research Your Major

College is a major decision in your life because there are so many great opportunities that await you after you receive your degree. College, for the most part, is the first time that many students become independent for their own success. College is different from high school because most decisions you must make are on your own. In college, you are able to pick your classes and times you would like to take those courses. It is a lot different from high school where you have a structured daily schedule that every student must follow. College schedules give you the ability to have large amounts of time in between your classes. Most students use that time for naps and other things that will entertain them. However, I feel that most of that free time should be used for studying because in college level courses, there is more material to digest, and you have to study on your own to prepare for assessments. If you get your work done first, there will be lots of free time for you to enjoy. I find it helpful to study my notes for 30 minutes directly after class and before I rest for the evening. I would advise students to have a balanced sleeping schedule because it will help keep you energized and focused in class.

In addition, if you are a student who gets homesick, try not to go home your first month of school because you have to get adjusted to being away from home. Doing this will allow you to make the transition a little easier and give you the opportunity to become more familiar with the campus and the surrounding area.

I would strongly advise students not to start any major assignments right before the due date. In high school, this is a major habit many students struggle with, but it's important to break this habit before college. College work adds up. You might have two to three projects at a time with all your classes combined. Waiting until the last minute to complete these projects could put you in jeopardy of not doing well. I would suggest completing all major projects 1 week before the due date because it will make your life a whole lot easier. Try to also set up a 9-to-5 schedule because it will help you prepare for your career after college.

Furthermore, make sure you do not waste any valuable study time. Before going to college, research facts and information about your major. Many professors expect students to come in with some knowledge on the subject at hand. It's always good to know more information beforehand so you will be prepared for assignments and have an upper hand over some of your fellow peers. Always be ready to defend your answers to certain questions and discussions in class because professors in college want you to be able to analyze and put things into perspective. Meet as many people as you can because you don't know what connections you can make along the way that will not only benefit you in college but also in your career after college.

Matthew

Symphony
Love

Patuxent High School, 2013

Key Points

1. Set Goals
2. Consider Financial Matters
3. ALWAYS Work to Max Potential
4. Find Your Interest

Everyone expects something different from their kid once he or she graduates; college may be an option or maybe even trade school. Every individual should have some sort of goal to work towards once he or she leaves high school. Being an independent student will get you further than being a follower. In other words, find what sparks YOUR interest, and RUN WITH IT! Looking to the left or right at the competition can break your focus and slow you down, so it is best to keep a clear, open mindset. College may not be for every person, but it is a good choice to consider. The main things that scare students away the most are financial worries. It is in every student's best interest to earn as many scholarships as you can, and apply for financial AID to help with the burden of education costs. Whichever path you decide to choose, make sure you follow your plans all the way through and ALWAYS work to your MAX POTENTIAL!

Riddicia
Mackall

Huntingtown High School, 2010
Howard University, 2014

Key Points

1. Grow Into the Person You are Meant to Be
2. Be Kind
3. Take Risks
4. Have Fun
5. Stick to Your Beliefs

"You have brains in your head. You have feet in your shoes. You can steer yourself any direction you choose." —Dr. Seuss

Your college experience is what you make of it. If I had to sum up my college experience into one word, it would be: Growth. Growing into the person who I was always destined to be. Challenging myself, whether it was in a classroom or a social setting. Building an everlasting network of diverse, yet like-minded individuals, whether it was professionally or personally. I learned to take advantage of all opportunities that were presented before me. As you are in the transition stages between teenager and an adult who pays bills on a regular basis, there is no better time than the time in college to try out anything your mind or heart is telling you to do. There were many hardships and failures, but one of the best parts of college is that you learn to become resilient and to persevere through any obstacle.

My advice: Be kind to others. Take risks, and try new things. Get comfortable with the uncomfortable. Know your worth. Stick strong to your own beliefs. Most importantly, have fun. With these things in mind, you're destined to grow into the person you are meant to become.

I wish the best in all of your endeavors.

Beth
Mead

Patuxent High School, 2014
Towson University

Key Points

1. Transferring May Enter Your Thoughts—Know When to Transfer

2. Balance—Step Out of Your Comfort Zone

3. Study Abroad

4. Discover Moments

I am currently a junior studying computer science at Towson University, and I am a proud graduate of Patuxent High School. I entered college as the first in my family; so, I felt a little more pressure to succeed. I first attended Notre Dame of Maryland University. After spending my freshman year there, I realized that I loved Baltimore, but Notre Dame was not the right school for me. I transferred to Towson University for my sophomore year and got off to a rough start. I had a hard time integrating myself into the much larger campus, making friends, and adjusting to the different learning style.

The first semester at Towson, my GPA dropped from a 3.7 to a 2.5. The grades hit me like water to the face. I realized I needed to be more diligent, more focused, and to balance my time. In hindsight, I would tell any transfer student to be careful, not to overestimate your previous A's and take for granted your rate of success. If you allow yourself to become distracted for even a moment, a bad habit can form, and you must work twice as hard to catch up. I also encourage joining a club of interest. A hobby can help you maintain a balance as well as connect with people who have the same interests. I joined ballroom dancing, and now, I dance every week with a great group of students. Don't be afraid to step out of your comfort zone either. It took me 4 months to join a club, but once I did, I regretted waiting so long to put myself out there.

My second piece of advice is to study abroad! I knew I wanted to travel the world since I was a child. I really started planning it when I was 16 and looking for universities. Within the first 2 months I was at Towson, I was looking into applications for study abroad.

I chose England, filled out the application, waited for acceptance, filled out scholarships for study abroad, and began my journey to Europe. There is something incredible to say about studying, living, submersing yourself into a different country. It speaks volumes of bravery, resilience, and passion for the world, not to mention employers love to see resumes and transcripts with study abroad experience. It takes a lot of effort and hard work, emotionally, physically, and financially, but if you want it, you can do it. I spent 3 months in Canterbury, England, at the University of Kent. It was spectacular! The time there alone could fill a book, but I also traveled to Scotland, Ireland, and four cities in France. Once you have traveled, the world has been put into perspective—yes, it is big, but it is anything you wish it to be. The cities, countries, and continents open to cultures, history, food (oh the food!) and people who illuminate a new path in your life. Around every corner is a moment to be discovered. I kept this attitude even when returning. Traveling is addicting….Once you do it, you cannot stop! Every study abroad trip is unique, but the new passion after experiencing it is always the same.

This is my first semester back after studying abroad. It is true what they say—you find a completeness and strength to continue studying. I am a lifelong learner and traveler. I have to finish strong now…. And if I decide on graduate school, I will apply to one in England.

Beth

Brandon Perkins

Gwynn Park High School, 2016
Allegany Community College

Key Points

1. Do Anything You Want
2. Have Fun but Work First, Fun Second
3. Bring Your "A" Game
4. Create Your Atmosphere and Environment

After graduating from Gwynn Park High School, I knew my life was going to change. The college I attend is Allegany Community College. When I started college last August, everything was new to me, everything was up to me, and I was considered as an adult. To be honest, college is the life! At Allegany, I have met a lot of new people and made new friends. The best part about college is that you can do anything you want and have fun. The things I experienced were the people, the atmosphere, the environment, and there's a lot of work to do. My first semester was really challenging. All of my classes had finals and projects, and everything was due around the same time, but I had everything under control.

My tip for students who are going to college is to be prepared when you're in college because college is no joke! You have to be on your "A" game and stay on your P's and Q's. I have seen a lot of students getting kicked out of college for slacking off. Remember work first, fun second.

Aleia **Plenty**

Calvert High School, 2014
Stevenson University

Key Points

1. Study What You Enjoy
2. Think Ahead
3. Make a List and Tour Colleges
4. Get Involved
5. Be Competitive
6. Consider Being a Resident Assistant
7. Get a Life Beyond the Dorm
8. Keep a Checklist of Goals

As a college student preparing for an early graduation followed by law school, I believe that I have some valuable advice for you at virtually any point in your education journey, whether you are beginning to look at colleges, heading off to college, or graduating from college. My advice is simple. What I have to say is straightforward and can be applied to any field of study.

Simply put, you have to study something that you truly enjoy. When you hit a rough patch, and you will hit a rough patch, this can be all that keeps you going. So when choosing colleges or majors, you must take the advice of others with a grain of salt; what is important to you may not be important to others. Personally, I made a list of all the schools that I was interested in based on price, location, reputation, and whether they had my field of study. Then, I made sure to tour all of them (this is so crucial!) to see the campuses firsthand. The quality and cleanliness of the dorms could (and did) make or break a school for me. Just ensure that you can actually picture yourself in that environment, and trust your intuition since you will be living there for 4 years.

It is also very important to always think ahead, and put yourself in the best position possible. Even as a college freshman, or even a high school junior, you should be thinking about the consequences of your actions, and create a checklist (mental or physical, it is up to you) of steps you must take to reach your ultimate goal. For example, if you are a high school junior and you know that you want to go to a school that has a reputation for doing a lot of community service, you may want to start being active in your community. Or, if you are a freshman in college trying to get your bearings but you know (or think) that you eventually want to go to graduate school or graduate with honors, you must maintain good grades and avoid giving anyone a reason to turn you away. This means that you must be as competitive as an applicant as possible. I find it helpful to constantly update and review my resume, looking for strengths and weaknesses; this paper essentially determines your future. Think of it as a way to see in yourself what your employers will see.

Included in putting yourself in the best position possible would be things like clubs, organizations, activities, and internships. The more stacked your resume is, the better. Even if you want to become a teacher, but you can only find an internship working in a financial aid office, take it. For one thing, you may stumble upon something you never thought you would like that can change your entire plans. Any experience in a professional setting will also benefit you regardless of what you want to do.

Lastly, **get involved!** I mentioned above some reasons why employers or future admissions committees will appreciate community involvement, but you should also do it for yourself. I have been a Resident Assistant on campus for 2 years, and I have found that time and time again, whenever my residents are unhappy or homesick, it is usually because they haven't found their niche. I even went through this my freshman year because I went to classes, came back to my dorm room, and studied—that was it. It was the most miserable experience, and I would not want anyone else to go through that. You want to feel connected and have a sense of belonging, which is easiest to do in your first year because everyone is looking to make friends.

Use college as an opportunity to expand mentally, spiritually, and socially. At this time, you experience rapid changes, which should be met with excitement and determination rather than fear. These years are some of the best of your life, and that is not to be taken for granted. You are destined for many great things. It is simply up to you whether you fulfill that destiny or not.

Aleia

Wilbur
Robinson

Calvert High School, 2016
College of Southern Maryland

Key Points

1. Do Not Abuse Freedom
2. Do Not Miss Classes
3. Set Deadlines
4. Sleep Is Important

My first semester of college was a fun and challenging experience. The atmosphere is different from high school because you are on your own, and what you do is completely on you now. I liked the freedom that I had gained, but knew that I should not abuse it, or I could risk failing. One of the challenges that I went through in the beginning was moving at the fast pace that each unit was taught. In high school, you have the whole year to learn a subject, but in college, you have only 15 weeks. Missing 1 day of class in college feels like missing almost a week of class in high school.

After wrapping up the semester, some advice to incoming freshmen would be to commit yourselves to getting your work done on time and meeting all the deadlines. If there is a subject that you know you are not strong in or want to guarantee a high grade, get a tutor early because it's better to get one before your grade begins to drop. Sleep is important. Make sure to get plenty of it, or getting up for class in the morning will be an everyday struggle. College is the next big step in life and is meant to be fun, but don't let having too much be a distraction.

Shala
Thomas

Northern High School, 2015
Hampton University, Sophomore

Key Points

1. Pre-College Activities are Recommended

2. Embrace the Diversity of Students

3. Speak Up

4. It's Okay to Make Mistakes

5. Realize It's Okay to Miss Home and Your Parents

College is not for everyone. Everyone has his or her own story and interpretation of college, but this is my story as a current second semester sophomore at Hampton University. My freshman year of college socially and academically was fearless, and I was in full control. I had the opportunity to spend 5 weeks on campus for Pre-College prior to my freshman year. My whole college experience molded me into the person I am today.

Pre-College is an early preparation for the fall semester of college. The weeks are filled with academics and socializing. The students take two or three classes 5 days a week, and all of the classes are 3 credits. Two or three classes sound easier than high school, but it is college. The pace is faster, and there is more temptation around.

I had been given advice and told horror stories about roommates. Those stories made me fearful of my future roommate. When I first met her, she was nice and polite. But I could hear an echo in my head repeating, "Don't trust your roommate. She is still a stranger." I locked all of my belongings. New surroundings are filled with strangers, but eventually strangers became my family. I met people from Chicago, Florida, New York, North Carolina, and other States. All of the different people who I met taught me many different things about myself that neither my parents nor my friends back home could teach me. The hardest part of Pre-College was when my parents finished unpacking my bags and loaded up the car to drive back to Maryland. I played it off really well, but on the inside I wanted to cry when they went back home. Within 2 days, my roommate and I were walking around campus introducing ourselves and meeting people on our dorm floor.

Within the 5 weeks, I had to stand up for myself with my friends and professors. I have learned that you have a mouth for a reason; so, speak up, and present yourself with class and respect because everyone can be watching you.

Even though I attended Pre-College, had developed relationships, and knew my way around campus, there was still room to grow.

My freshman year was not perfect. I made plenty of mistakes and lost friends back home and on campus. College is a wonderful experience, but you have to be careful of the company you keep because your friends are a reflection of you. I would tell the incoming freshmen to enjoy your 4 years of college because the real world is coming soon. The most challenging thing is time management. But you must get involved in activities. I was a member of the Chorus, attended the Dr. William R. Harvey Leadership Institute, was a Resident Assistant, a Contributing Editor for the H*ampton Script* as well the *Maryland Daily Examiner*, and was on the Dean's List.

You must prioritize the importance of education.

Shala

Tiffany
Toye

Calvert High School, 2011
Morgan State University, 2015

Key Points

1. Always Be Yourself
2. Apply for Scholarships
3. Graduate
4. Discover Yourself
5. Keep God First
6. Just Breathe

Going to college was one of the most exciting and scariest decisions I have ever made. I was most afraid of the unknowns. How is living away from home? How am I going to pay for college? What if I don't make friends? All of these questions continually ran through my mind. I sought knowledge from mentors and peers who had gone through the experience. They advised me to always be myself and always remember why I was in college. The ultimate goal was to graduate!

College is a journey. I discovered a lot about myself. As a young Christian woman, I found that my faith was often tested. While I did not pass every test, I knew the importance of keeping God first in my life. My faith and spiritual beliefs are the only reasons I made it through the journey.

To all future college students, there are going to be moments of unimaginable stress, but remember to just breathe. Always keep God first, and try not to procrastinate. Lastly, get as many scholarships as you can.

Best Wishes.

Nicole
Cooksey

President, Concerned Black Women
Morgan State University, 2000
Webster University's George Herbert Walker School of
**   Business, 2011 & 2012**

Key Points

1. Prepare for Homesickness

2. Transferring May Enter Your Thoughts

3. Don't Stress Over Your First Bad Grade

4. Network

One of my favorite times of the year is graduation season when there are so many excited high school seniors who will soon be heading off to college. College is one of the most exciting times of a young person's life, and seeing that joy brings me to a nostalgic place because I truly enjoyed my collegiate experience. While this experience was one I fondly recall, that does not mean that there were not challenges to overcome. I always like to tell students as they enter their first year of college that these are a magical 4 years that can never be recreated. Enjoy the struggles along with the fantastic times that come along with college life. I am sure that if you are reading this as a newly graduated senior you cannot imagine anything except the awesome new opportunities that await you. However, if you are a seasoned sophomore, junior, or senior, you know some of the fun and not so enjoyable moments that encompass college life. Hopefully, the following words will provide you with a guide if any of these situations prove true for you.

As a graduating senior at Morgan State University in 2000, I did not get an opportunity to reflect on all the lessons I had learned in and out of the classrooms. But as a professional and community activist who now frequently speaks to students on the importance of higher education, there are mainly four lessons that I tend to impart as worthy advice. The lessons are: One, most students, even when they do not think they ever will, miss home. Two, the urge to transfer usually crosses most students minds a few times during the first semester. Three, do not stress out about the first bad grade that you receive. Four, make the most of your 4 years by networking as much as possible.

Most students, no matter how excited to move away from home, at some point will likely become homesick. Typically, this feeling starts to set in after the "honeymoon phase" is over, and the real work of classes, writing papers, and taking tests have begun. The overwhelming sense that nothing is going the way it should, and the feeling that you don't quite fit into the college campus that you loved a few weeks ago is weighing heavily on you. You feel as if you need to go home just to be around familiar surroundings and things that are comfortable. Don't worry. More than half of your friends attending other colleges and fellow classmates feel exactly the same way. There is nothing wrong with being homesick, and hopefully, you are attending school close enough to home so that you can visit for Thanksgiving to get a good dose of your family's unconditional love to power you through the rest of the semester. If by chance you are attending school far from home and your parents or guardians can only bring you home after the semester ends, try things like FaceTime or Skype, go to a good friend's home for the weekend, or even speak to a counselor to help you feel better. It's okay to miss home, and believe me, everyone at home is missing you too.

Something that goes hand in hand with homesickness is the urge to transfer. Thoughts of transferring usually occur because of reminders of all the colleges that were located closer to home, bad grades that were not expected, or maybe you have realized that the big university that you thought you would love, really doesn't fit your personality. A bit of advice on this touchy subject would be to really assess your feelings on why you want to transfer to another school. Remember that this is most likely the first time you have been away from home and provided with time that is all your own, and, you have no one to tell you to go study or to get your homework done. All of these things will still occur at any school. Talk to your parents, a counselor, or a professor about your rationale, and truly listen to the feedback they have for you. Transferring is a big step—one you do not want to take purely on emotions.

Many students reading this guide will have enjoyed a successful A-average high school career with minimal studying or excessive hard work. I always tell students that those high school straight A's do not transfer over to college. The rigor is set at a different level, which creates an environment that the level of study required in high school does not compete with. The key to combating this issue is to realize more is now being required of you. Rise to the occasion instead of letting your first bad grade become an all-encompassing stressful situation. Learn better study habits. Realize that time management is very important. And remember if you are the smartest person in your study group you are helping everyone else, which is great, but you should also find another group in which you are not the smartest in order to raise your own performance level.

Lastly, while you are in college, you should certainly be networking. Everyone you meet has been put in your path for a reason. Either for you to be of help, or for them to help you. Being a blessing to someone else usually becomes a blessing for yourself. Within your 4 years of undergraduate college, you will need tutoring, summer jobs, internships, all of which can be obtained by networking with your fellow classmates, professors, and administrators.

Remember that the four years of undergraduate school is THE most magical time of your life. Enjoy every moment of it because you will never have another period quite as special. Work hard to play hard; keep your mind focused on the fact that your first priority is school and to make great grades so that you can do all of the fun things that come along with college. Pray and stay busy. I know you will be great, and if no one else has told you, I am proud of you!

Old-School Reflections

Rhonda
Thomas

President, LEAP Forward, Inc.
Tennessee State University, 1980
University of Southern California, 1982
University of Pennsylvania, 1985

Key Points

1. Make Sacrifices
2. Be Prepared When Opportunities Come
3. You Have to Pay Your Success Forward

My journey into the engineering field began my senior year at Calvert High School. While walking down a hallway, I just happened to see one of the high school counselors, Mr. Wallace Lorenzo Leeper. He stopped me and asked if I was prepared for life after graduation. I replied, "yes," and gleefully expressed my plans to attend my first college choice, Norfolk State University, and major in English with a concentration in journalism. I always knew I wanted to attend an out-of-state Historically Black College and University (HBCU).

During my teen years, I was fascinated with Langston Hughes, a prolific Harlem Renaissance writer who captured my heart with his poetry, short stories, and novels I borrowed from the mobile library that came through my neighborhood during the summers. It was because of my love for Hughes' writing that I also desired to write. However, my future would take a different turn.

Mr. Leeper asked me what I would do with an English degree, and I replied that I would teach until I could get my journalism career started. He actually said to me, "Why do you want to do that? Teachers don't make much money." This was in the late 1970s and sadly, his statement still rings true today. He pointed out my completed math and science classes and suggested that with my academic background perhaps I should consider an engineering career. (Even though I finished Geometry with a "D!")

What is ironic is that I did not even know what an engineer was and had never been introduced to this career field. He briefly explained the role of an engineer and stated that he was actively recruiting for an engineering program that specifically trained and educated minority students. The program was based in St. Mary's County at the Naval Air Test Center in Patuxent River, Maryland. The U.S. Department of the Navy was making an effort to increase the number of minority students pursuing technical degrees and careers. The program provided college financial assistance and employment during the summers to work alongside engineering professionals to obtain actual hands-on experience.

I trusted Mr. Leeper's judgment, and we began the process for my admission. Regardless of my lack of exposure to technical careers, my counselor wanted me to capitalize on my academic background and was determined that I get into this cooperative education program called Pax-Tenn— Pax for Patuxent River and Tenn because of the partnership with Tennessee State University (TSU) in Nashville, Tennessee.

I remember it just as if it was yesterday how he marched me into his office, asked me the questions, and then wrote my responses on the application. Mr. Leeper submitted the application, and we waited. After interviewing, I was accepted into the program. And yes, they asked about my "D" in geometry during the interview! My reply was that it was an answer to my prayers.

Being the first in my immediate family to attend college, I really applied myself. I was afraid to fail because too many people were depending on my success, including Mr. Leeper, who maintained contact with me. Unfortunately, Mr. Leeper, a young man in his 40s, lost his battle with cancer while I was still in college.

His efforts were not in vain. I successfully completed the program and received a Bachelor of Science Degree in Electrical Engineering, becoming the first African American woman to graduate from the Pax-Tenn Program, and I began working for the Navy Department.

As I reflect on my college experiences at TSU, I am glad that I chose a HBCU. The teachers were very nurturing, all the students were willing to help each other, and we had many study sessions together. Everyone just wanted everyone else to do well.

I am a true believer in education because I know no one can take it from you. During my Navy Department years, my advanced degrees were also funded, as I earned a Master of Science Degree in Systems Management from the University of Southern California (USC) and a Master of Science Degree in Systems Engineering from the University of Pennsylvania (PENN).

I recall that USC rejected me at first because of my low Graduate Record Exam scores, and I challenged their decision. I questioned why they would use one criterion instead of looking at all of my credentials——the bigger picture. I was eventually accepted, began work on my master's degree, and finished with a 3.45 GPA.

After completing the Systems Management program a year later, I applied for an educational program on the campus of PENN with my full tuition paid and a continued salary from the Navy. My experiences at PENN were very different from my HBCU experiences. I was not nurtured, and I struggled. I didn't feel as if I belonged, and it was hard. I was even placed on academic probation at one point, used tutors, and repeated a withdrawn Control Theory class. It was during this experience that my true relationship with God commenced and grew stronger. Struggles will define what you are made of.

When you are used to A's and B's, it hurts when you don't live up to your own expectations. Once, after an exam paper was returned, I folded it, put it away, and did not look at it until I returned home. I sort of felt as if I had performed sufficiently. However, when I got home and looked at my grade, it was a score of 17, and that was not out of 20 but 17/100. I cried crocodile tears that night, but also decided that I needed a tutor to stay on course.

I also remember completing my last semester on PENN's campus but still needing one more class to graduate. Yes, it was my repeat Control Theory class. My education was funded for 1 year with the Navy. I returned home, degreeless but determined to finish. I enrolled in that class and paid for it on my own. It was a Tuesday 7:00 pm to 10:00 pm class. I would get in my car on every Tuesday and drive from Lexington Park, Maryland to Philadelphia, Pennsylvania to take this class, and after class, drive back home and make it to work the next day. I am grateful that God saw my sacrifice.

I remember after the final exam going to the professor's office to have my work graded right then. I think I received an 85, a high B. He said if I waited until he graded the other papers, he would probably grade on a curve, and my grade could be higher. I replied that I was satisfied with my grade. You see, my prayer was to graduate, and the minimum requirement for graduation was a 3.0 GPA. The exam grade gave me exactly a cumulative 3.0 GPA—the answer to my prayer.

I have learned that sometimes opportunity will knock at your door (such as with my divine encounter with Mr. Leeper in a hallway), and then other times, you will need to go out and create an opportunity to ensure your success. The key is being prepared when opportunities occur.

In observing my community surroundings in Calvert County, I noticed how many minority youth in my rural county did not seem motivated to want any more in life other than jobs at the local Wal-Mart. I surmised that they were not realizing their full potential, and I was saddened by that discovery and decided to take action.

On the heels of my success, I was determined that I would be the face of engineering for other underrepresented students. I convinced some of my friends (Wilhemina, Conrad, Maurice, Timothy, Robert, Wilson, and Burdette) from the Pax-Tenn era to help also, and the nonprofit, LEAP Forward, Inc.—appropriately named after the man who had allowed God to use him to guide my path—was born in 1998. A scholarship program existed in Mr. Leeper's memory, but it was struggling and Mr. Russell Costley, another educator in the Calvert County School System, provided guidance.

We committed our own resources to improving the lives of other students. To champion this cause, initially, we spoke to students in elementary, middle, and high schools about attending college and pursuing engineering careers; took them out of the county to visit college campuses; and we helped students complete applications, essays, and financial aid materials. In addition, through LEAP Forward, we provided scholarships and other financial support for admission applications and test fees, and introduced students to programs sponsored by professional organizations, such as the Society of Women Engineers, the National Society of Black Engineers (NSBE), and the Black Engineers of the Year Awards Conference. To date, LEAP Forward representatives have spoken to hundreds of youth about science, technology, engineering and math (STEM) career paths, the rewards and satisfaction of obtaining a degree, and the fulfillment that comes from doing the work you love. I am pleased to say that LEAP Forward has awarded over 100 scholarships to help students reach their education goals and potential.

Because of Mr. Leeper's guidance and belief in me in high school, I know firsthand that a little direction and encouragement can go a long way. I have chosen to follow his lead and to perform a similar community service. Today, working with youth has become my passion.

Wallace Lorenzo Leeper
1935-1978

Rhonda's Words of Advice to Students:

- Always remember Jeremiah 29:11. "For I know the plans I have for you, declares the LORD, plans to prosper you and not to harm you, plans to give you hope and a future."

- Talk to Your Counselors and Get All the Advice You Can.

- Education Is Important—Really Apply Yourself.

- Prepare for Opportunities.

- Find Students Willing to Help You—Study with Them—Grow with Them.

- Speak Up for Yourself—Do Not Be Defined by Standardized Tests.

- Academic Probation Is a Wakeup Call Not a Death Sentence.

- There Is No Shame in Needing a Tutor—Ask for Help.

- Crying Is a Great Release. After the Tears, Get Back to Work.

- A Bad Exam Score Is a Signal that You Need Help—Get It.

- Never Underestimate the Power of Determination.

- Sometimes You Will Have to Make Sacrifices. But It Will All Work Out.

- Keep a Cheerleader Handy—Someone Who Will Encourage You Along Your Journey.

- When You Hear a Voice Say, No Way, You Reply, YES, There Is a Way, and You Make It Happen.

- Find a Way to Give Back to Others.

- God Is with You During the Sunshine and the Storms—**Do NOT** Stop Praying. God Infuses Our Lives with Purpose, Meaning, and Joy.

- Make Your First Semester Your Best Semester. Your GPA Is Cumulative, and Your "Base" Grades (First Semester Grades) Will Determine Your Foundation. Example: First Semester, 3.50 and Second Semester, 2.50. Cumulative, GPA 3.0. Your First Semester's Performance Provides a Cushion. Make Your Studies Priority One. Establish a Good Foundation—a Good Base.

- Encourage Yourself Each Day. Make a Sign, Place It on Your Mirror So You See It, and Recite It Each Morning. Example: "Good Morning Jackie Door. In May 2025, I Will Graduate with a B.S. Degree in Mechanical Engineering," or Something Like This—"Good Morning Jack Wall— Future Mechanical Engineer. You Can Do This!"

- When Faced with Challenges, Your Perspective Will Drive Your Reaction. What Do You See an Open Door or Obstacles? Have a Good Attitude.

- Ask for Help If You Need It. There is No Shame in Getting Help. Seek a Tutor. "F" Really Does Not Mean Failure. It Means Learn the Lesson—Get Help.

- Surround Yourself with People Who Will Encourage You to Study and Not Party.

- Do Your Best. That is All That Can Be Expected of You—Your Best.

- Visit Your Professors. Let Them Get to Know You.

- ✓ If You Are Looking for Additional Financial Aid, Visit the Financial Aid Office. Introduce Yourself. Ask If There Are Any Unclaimed Scholarships. Maybe the Student Chose Another University. Always Ask If There Are New Scholarship Opportunities.

- ✓ If You Are Going to Choose Work Study, Try to Request It in Your Department of Concentration, i.e., Education, Engineering, Nursing.

- ✓ College Relationships Last a Lifetime. Expand Your Horizons. Get to Know Students Outside of Your Academic Department.

- ✓ This Will Be the Best Time of Your Life—You Will Get Out of College What You Put in.

- ✓ Sit in the "T" for Every Class. The "T" Includes the Front Rows and in the Seats in the Middle. This Tends to Be the Professor's Eye Focus Area.

- ✓ If You Have Situations Where You Feel You Are Being Treated Unfairly, Tell a Parent, Mentor, Or University Officials So That They Can Be Your Advocate.

- ✓ You Have a Voice. There Would Be No Universities or Professors without Your Tuition. They Are There to Serve You with an Education.

- ✓ Time Management Will Be Important. Use an App or Some Tool to Help You Stay on a Schedule. Schedule Classes. Schedule Reading, Free, and Relaxation Time.

- ✓ Think Three Times Before You Make Choices. Give Yourself 24 hours To Make Decisions. Bad Choices Have Consequences.

- ✓ Your Body Is Your Temple. You Can Have a Good Time Without Alcohol and Drugs. There Is Only "ONE" You. Most Jobs Will Require Background Checks and Questionnaires. You Want to Be Able to Answer Honestly.

- ✓ Remember Your College Performance Determines: What Type of Employment You Will Be Able to Obtain, What Type of Lifestyle You Will Be Able to Live, What Type of House You Will Be Able to Afford, What Type of Car You Will Drive, and on and on. Your Education Determines the Quality of Life You Will Live.

- ✓ Fraternities and Sororities Are Good Social Networks. Do Not Sacrifice Your Grades And Well-being. There are Graduate Level Opportunities for Joining.

Rhonda

Organizations' Background

Launching Educational Assistance Programs Forward, Incorporated also known as **LEAP Forward**, Inc. is a nonprofit organization that is poised to inspire, engage, educate and expose youth to a better and productive future. Even before the organization was recognized by the U.S. Internal Revenue Service as a 501 3(c) nonprofit in 2001, LEAP Forward started providing services in 1998 when the first three scholarships were awarded. Over 100 scholarships have been presented to students who have demonstrated academic prowess and financial need.

LEAP Forward is passionately committed to helping youth make better life and career choices; encouraging youth to excel in school, by promoting science, technology, engineering, and math (STEM) careers; and striving to increase the participation of underrepresented youth in the technological jobs pipeline.

We conduct a vigorous outreach program to educate and **expose** youth to STEM opportunities via engineering camps, conferences, exhibits and presentations; escort students to colleges and universities to interface with collegiate students and experience college life; and provide networking for graduates eager to enter into the workforce.

What is at the forefront of our hearts is the need for LEAP Forward to give back to our youth. How can we in good conscience sit back and be satisfied with "ourselves" and turn our backs on our youth? We cannot.

Our services include but are not limited to:

- Science, Technology, Engineering and Math Literacy and Exposure—NSBE Jr. Chapter Creative and Striving Hard to Succeed
- Academic Enrichment and Reinforcement
- Encouragement and Motivation
- Tutoring—Your Education Serves
- Mentoring—Destined "4" Success
- Professional Career Guidance and Growth
- College Admissions Process Navigation
- Scholarships and Other Financial Assistance

We want to leave the world a better place by creating future generations of LEAPERS. Students who:

Learn all they can

Excel beyond their own belief

Achieve consistently in their schoolwork

Perform as best they can

Explore new subjects, places, ideas

Rise to the next challenge

Thank you to past and present LEAP Forward Board Members, Family, Friends, Volunteers, Advisors, Supporters and all Students Who Pay It Forward

CONTACT INFORMATION

Website: www.leapforwardinc.org

Email: leapforwardinc@yahoo.com

Twitter: @leapforwardleap

Combined Federal Campaign (CFC) #91127

Amazon smile—smile.amazon.com/ch/52-2169397

Facebook: LEAP Forward Inc. and Calvert County NSBE Jr. CASH

Instagram: #leapforward2

LEAP Forward Family Scholarships Past and Present:

Wallace LEEPER

Dorothy Mae SMITH

Elizabeth SIMMS

Marilyn Preston KILLINGHAM

Vivian ROGERS

Michael MOORE

Earl THORNE

Raymond HARRIS

Clifton MORSELL/Randolph ADAMS

Violet PARKER

Hamilton and Alice PARRAN

Gloria Mae GROSS

Gladys HENSON

Lawrence MYERS

Iris HARRIS

George and Geneva Green HARROD

Wilson ENNIS, Sr.

Billy FINCH

Blanche FINCH

Nannie Pearl Taylor CADE

Evelyn IRVINE

Grace PARKER

Pamela OFFER

MacArthur JONES

Ruth REID

Fernande PERSONNA

THOMAS Family

Carrie Bertha JONES – In Celebration of Clyde JONES

VICTORIA LODGE #71

Thank you Families for Sponsoring Scholarships. What an impact you have made to our youth. May the memory of your loved one live on through your generosity.

Thank you to past and present LEAP Forward Board Members. The vision came to pass because you help execute the plan. We may never know all the lives we influenced.

Thank you to ALL our Financial Contributors and Donors—you are investing in the futures of our youth.

Thank you Student Contributors. This book was not possible without your messages and advice. Thank you for paying it forward and having a desire to help those climbing the ladder of success behind you. We Love You All Just For Saying, "YES, I Will Help."

Thank you Rhonda Saunders of RS Graphx, Inc. for coming to our rescue and delivering a great layout. Your time and dedication to this book and our youth is truly appreciated.

Thank God for the Vision for "From Whence We Came," for the inspiration and guidance of His Spirit and for providing the resources to make this happen.

LEAP Forward, Inc.
Past Scholarship Recipients

1998 Scholarship Recipients
Kristen A. Taylor – Calvert High School
Johnny Coates – Northern High School
Gordon Taylor III – Calvert High School

1999 Scholarship Recipients
Terrell Ennis – Northern High School
Joanita Gross – Calvert High School
Danielle Johnson – Northern High School
Brandon King – Northern High School

2000 Scholarship Recipients
Lynette Johnson – Calvert High School

2001 Scholarship Recipients
Rebecca Fields – Calvert High School
Tiffany Gray – Patuxent High School
Larry Mackall – Patuxent High School
Patrick Robinson – Calvert High School
Kirby Spence – Great Mills High School

2002 Scholarship Recipients
Leeann Nicole Bryant – Calvert High School
Shalonda Hope Chew – Calvert High School
William J. Colbert, Jr. – Northern High School
Ralph Gray, Jr. – Calvert High School
Stacy Goldring – Patuxent High School
Chante R. Jones – Calvert High School

2003 Scholarship Recipients
Vasmin Natascha Edwards – Calvert High School
De'Maris Renee' Hannon – Calvert High School
Tiffany Shanae Norman – Lackey High School
Shionta Wyquila Pumphroy – Calvert High School

2004 Scholarship Recipients
Jessica Brooks – Calvert High School
Candeia Holland – Calvert High School
Alexis Howard – Fairfax Baptist Temple Academy
Quindara King – Great Mills High School
Charise Watts – Calvert High School

2005 Scholarship Recipients
Raymond Abad – Great Mills High School
Montell Rothwell – Patuxent High School
Justin Stepney – Calvert High School
Tiffany Caldwell – Great Mills High School
Ebony Charmaine Williams – Cardozo High School

2006 Scholarship Recipients
Tashrya A. Jones – Calvert High School
Dominique Reid – School Without Walls
Terrance M. Hall-Sutton – Calvert High School
Shoron Waul – Calvert High School
Nicole C. Greenfield – Calvert High School

2007 Scholarship Recipients
Kendra A. Edwards – Patuxent High School
Jermaine Mason – Calvert High School
Gerard Steven Muschette – Calvert High School
Courtney A. Sutton – Calvert High School

2008 Scholarship Recipients
Dynika Gross – Huntingtown High School
Jhalita Holland – Calvert High School
Ashley Jerre Jones – Calvert High School
LaQuita Jones – Calvert High School
Ashley Nicole Lindsey – Great Mills High School
Eugene Plater III – Huntingtown High School
Quonte Stewart – Calvert High School

2009 Scholarship Recipients
Michelle Brooks – Calvert High School
Jo'nel Roxanne Barnes – Calvert High School
Jasmin Nicole Brown – Calvert High School
Kelsey Edwards – Patuxent High School
Michael Ellison – Baltimore Polytechnic Institute
Jameela Hendricks – Baltimore Polytechnic Institute
Nalynn Y. Holland – Huntingtown High School
Ameellah S. Isley – Calvert High School
Jay Little, Jr. – Baltimore Polytechnic Institute

2010 Scholarship Recipients

Jasmine Adams – Northern High School
Kyle Hutzler – Huntingtown High School
Sharnice Long – Calvert High School
Devin Harrington – Baltimore Polytechnic Institute
Anitra Brooks – Calvert High School
Caira Cartwright – Home Schooled
Keiva Cole – Baltimore Polytechnic Institute
Monica Dureja – Northern High School
Shaunice Fenwick – Great Mills High School
Dai Quan Garner – Calvert High School
Breanna Harrod – Patuxent High School
Marcus Holland-Combs – Huntingtown High School
Ashley Madariaga – Northern High School
Crystal Trice – Calvert High School

2011 Scholarship Recipients

Kelsey Edwards – Patuxent High School
Riddicia Mackall – Huntingtown High School
Jordan Wilson – Northern High School
Sonya Crane – Northern High School
Tiffany Toye – Calvert High School
Jared Adam – Huntingtown High School
Tyler Austin – Patuxent High School
Turquoise Biscoe – Calvert High School
Daneya Boyd – Patuxent High School
Tierra Cooke – Calvert High School
Randl Dent – Northern High School
Shameka Harvey – Calvert High School
Pierce Jordan – Huntingtown High School
Travon Long – Calvert High School
Latara Swann – Calvert High School
Malik Tonkins – Northern High School
Dashawn Torney – Huntingtown High School
Ranesse Tyler – Calvert High School
Briana Wilkerson – Huntingtown High School

2012 Scholarship Recipients

Darius Jones – Patuxent High School
Riddicia Mackall – Huntingtown High School
Shakira Chapman – Calvert High School
Lachelle Stewart – Calvert High School
Torez Cooke – Calvert High School
Michael Greene – Baltimore Polytechnic Institute
Brittany Brown – Huntingtown High School
Tonique Butler – Calvert High School
Markeisha Creek – Calvert High School
Sylvester Phillips – Calvert High School
Jalen Scalyes – Calvert High School

2013 Scholarship Recipients

Brittany Brown – Huntingtown High School
Karrah Findley – Calvert High School
Kortina Moore – Patuxent High School
Symphony Love – Patuxent High School
Raneese Tyler – Calvert High School
Torez Cooke – Calvert High School
Danielle Deville – Patuxent High School
Erik Haskell II – Patuxent High School
Keisha Capers – Calvert High School
Matthew Doxie – Patuxent High School
Eric Gross – Patuxent High School
Malaysia Johnson – Calvert High School
Kaitlyn Torney – Patuxent High School

2014 Scholarship Recipients

Juwan Hawkins – Huntingtown High School
Martese Johnson – Patuxent High School
A'Miya Williams – Patuxent High School
Dillon Longo – Calvert High School
Reika Haskell – Northern High School
Malik Washington – Patuxent High School
Eric Gross – Patuxent High School
Kadesha Mitchell – Calvert High School
Anthony Jefferson – Calvert High School
Beth Mead – Patuxent High School
Kevin Jackson, Jr. – Patuxent High School
Simone Nicholes – Calvert High School
Jabrena Milburn – Chopticon High School
Iysha Dent – Northern High School
Trinity Mitchell – Huntingtown High School
Kayla Bush – Calvert High School

2015 Scholarship Recipients
Sydney Buckmire – Calvert High School
Breona Buck – Calvert High School
Ryan Adams – Northern High School
Joseph Berry III – Calvert High School
Shala Thomas – Northern High School
Monae Mackall – Calvert High School
Joshua Bell – Calvert High School
Autumn James – Huntingtown High School
Chardee Gross – Huntingtown High School
Karissa Fenwick – Patuxent High School
Brianna Mason – Calvert High School
Madison Tonic – Calvert High School
Kailyn Hutchins – Calvert High School
Raesha Estep – Calvert High School

2016 Scholarship Recipients
Jamal Holtz – Friendship Collegiate Academy
Aniya El-Wahhabi – Patuxent High School
Jerrell Jones – Northern High School
Jonathan Parks – Northern High School
Andre Jones – Calvert High School
Ryan Briggs – Northern High School
Dominique Jenkins – Patuxent High School
Chardenae Butler – Patuxent High School
Sha Niesha Johnson – Calvert High School
Trayonna Hutchins – Huntingtown High School
Jordyn Taylor – Huntingtown High School
Jaquan Kelley – Patuxent High School
Wilbur Robinson – Calvert High School
Cedric Fowler – Calvert High School
Isaiah Lewis – Annapolis High School
Dana Wiggins – Huntingtown High School
Taylor Jackson – Patuxent High School
Oluwaseyi Kintunde – Patuxent High School

2017 Scholarship Recipients
Aiyonna White – Northern High School
Cierra Morsell – Northern High School
Nia Adams – Northern High School
Nehemiah Stewart – Huntingtown High School
Kevin Wright – Northern High School
Sydney Slappy – Patuxent High School
Marcus Pratt Phelps – ACE High School
Sydney Houston – Patuxent High School
Alex Fletcher – Frederick Douglas High School
Zoe Walker – Huntingtown High School
Davaugh Reid – Huntingtown High School
Derrice Smith – Patuxent High School
Harleigh White – Huntingtown High School
Isaiah Ridley – Calvert High School
Marquise Bodley – Calvert High School
Brenae Mcleish – Calvert High School
Kalaya Hodges – Calvert High School
Lauren Cunningham – Northern High School
Trinity Parker – Patuxent High School
Alexis Adams – Northern High School
Dia Brown – Huntingtown High School
Ananda Claggett – Northern High School
Imani Watson – Calvert High School
Kevin Creek – Northern High School
Quenterrius Mason – Huntingtown High School

The **Concerned Black Women (CBW)** is a problem-solving and advocacy group using programmatic action, dissemination of information, networking to connect people in need with resources and services, cultural influence by sharing our heritage and its impact on today's society, and training and personal development.

Our services include but are not limited to:
- Service to the Calvert County community
- Establishment of scholarship programs
- Public leadership development and
- Participation in the governmental decision making process

The CBW held its first organizing meeting in June 2004. The organization was incorporated, in July, in the State of Maryland. The organization's founders are Doris J. Spencer and the late Annette J. Funn, two community activists who asked themselves the question, "Who is speaking on a variety of issues from the African American perspective?" They realized a need, and the rest is history.

CBW's mission is to address issues in the community that include education, health, economic well-being, and improving the quality of life for African American women and their families. We are working to change the life trajectory of families in Calvert County.

CBW's services include, but are not limited to, adult and youth mentoring programs, information technology training and access to decrease the Digital Divide, identification of health needs and issues, identification of special education issues, establishment of scholarship programs, development of youth and young adult leaders, and participation in the Local and State government decision-making process.

In addition, CBW provides four annual scholarships to African American High School Seniors who are graduating from Calvert County Public High Schools in Maryland and will be attending Institutions of Higher Learning. A scholarship will be given to one student at each of the four public high schools. Scholarships are awarded based on scholastic achievement, financial need, written essays, and school and community involvement. The scholarship can be used to pay for tuition, fees, books, or any collegiate needs.

Contact Information
Website: www.cbwcc.org
Email: cbwofcc@gmail.com
Facebook: @CBWCalCo
Twitter: @ConcernBlackWom
AmazonSmile: http://smile.amazon.com/ch/20-1333798

Concerned Black Women Past Scholarship Recipients

2006 Scholarship Recipients
Faith Holland – Huntingtown High School
Terrance Sutton – Calvert High School
Starr Hawkins – Patuxent High School

2007 Scholarship Recipients
Courtney Sutton – Calvert High School
Leonard S. Greene, Jr. – Huntingtown High School

2008 Scholarship Recipients
Glenn W. Ford, Jr. – Patuxent High School
Marissa Miller – Huntingtown High School
Charnell Bourne – Calvert High School
Dynika Gross – Huntingtown High School

2009 Scholarship Recipients
Danielle Newman – Northern High School
Nalynn Holland – Huntingtown High School
Chamainc Jones – Calvert High School

2010 Scholarship Recipients
Samantha Jones – Northern High School
Breanna Harrod – Patuxent High School
Riddicia Mackall – Huntingtown High School
Zackary Johnson – Calvert High School

2011 Scholarship Recipients
Sonya Crane – Northern High School
Chantelle Beachum – Patuxent High School
Christa Allen – Huntingtown High School
Latara Swann – Calvert High School

2012 Scholarship Recipients
Diamond Jones – Northern High School
Alesha Leonard – Patuxent High School
Cecilia Sanders – Huntingtown High School
LaChelle Stewart – Calvert High School

2013 Scholarship Recipients
Kaitlyn Torney – Patuxent High School
Jasmine Weems – Calvert High School
Michaela Miller – Huntingtown High School

2014 Scholarship Recipients
Aleia Plenty – Calvert High School
London Mackall – Huntingtown High School
Cecille Broussard – Calvert High School
Martese Johnson – Patuxent High School

2015 Scholarship Recipients
Joshua Bell – Calvert High School
Jai Horsey – Northern High School
Jadea Deahl – Patuxent High School
Jonathan Foster – Huntingtown High School

2016 Scholarship Recipients
ShaNiesha Johnson – Calvert High School
Elise Hopkins – Huntingtown High School
Jerrell Jones – Northern High School
Alexya Brown – Patuxent High School

2017 Scholarship Recipients
Imani Watson – Calvert High School
Nehemiah Stewart – Huntingtown High
Aiyonna White – Northern High School
Sydney Houston – Patuxent High School

Art Work by Sir Shadow – Education Matters

www.sirshadow.com

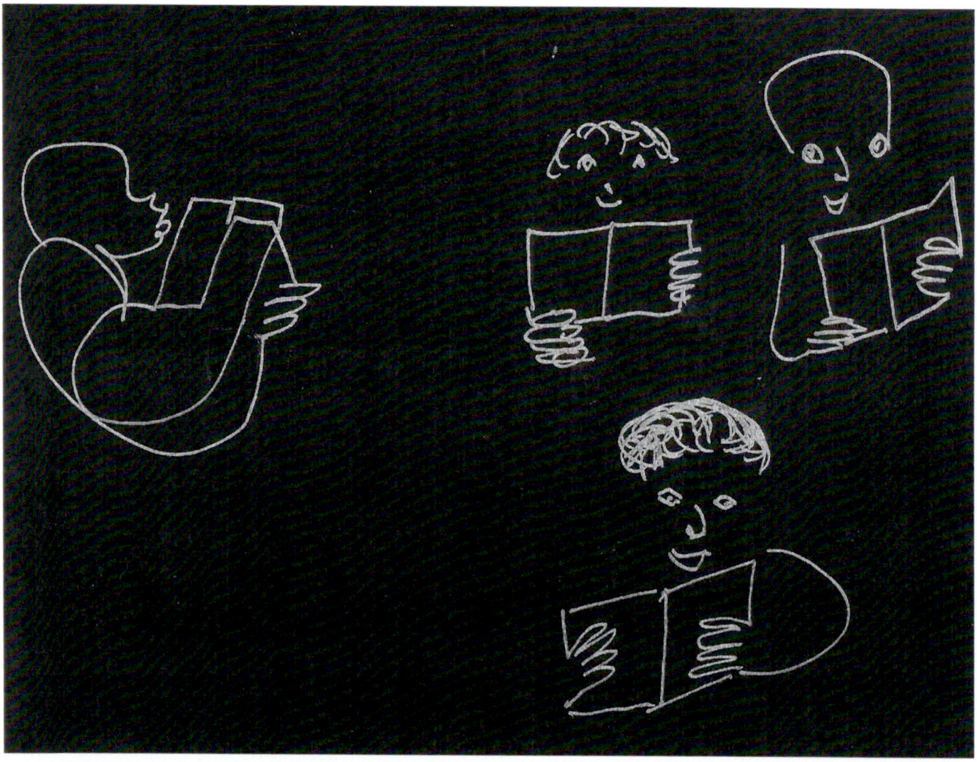

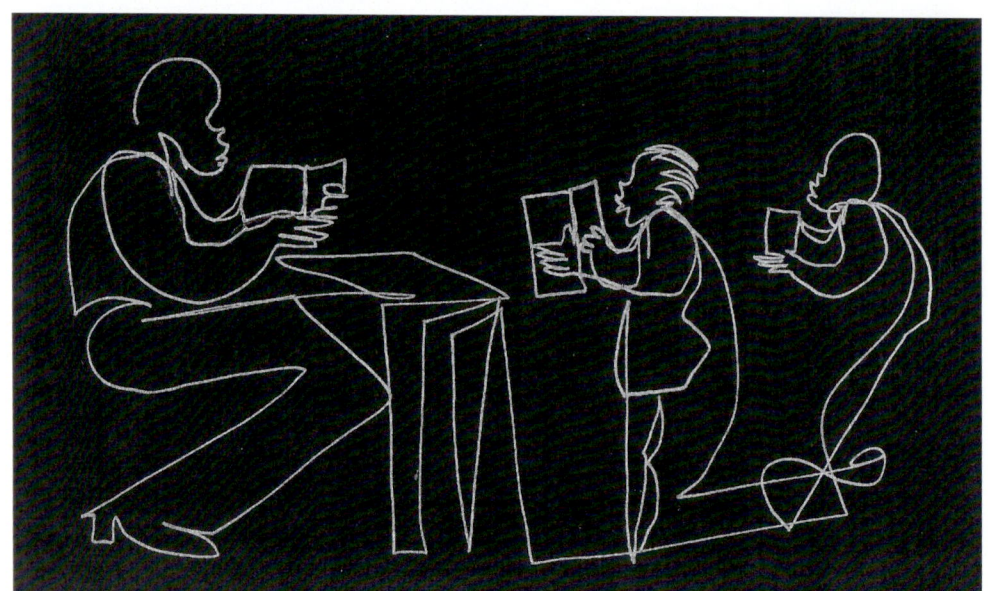

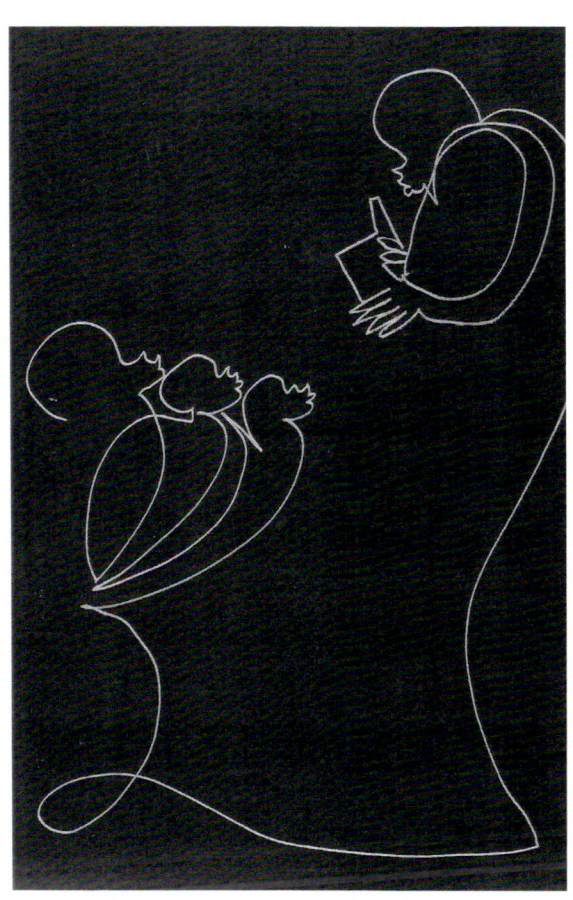

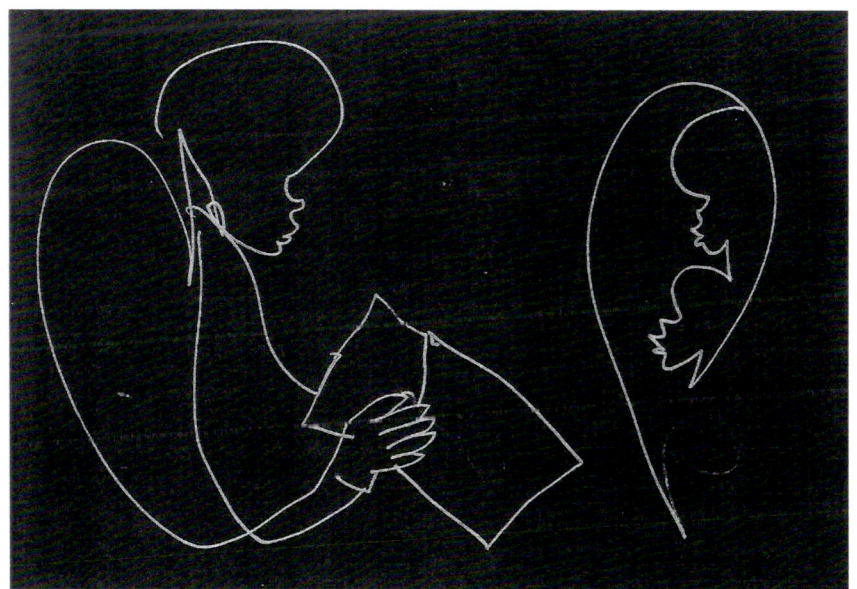

Comments

WE WANT TO HEAR FROM OUR READERS

If this book has provided you with needed tools for your educational journey and if you would like to share your college message, please email us at
<u>fromwhencewecamethebook@gmail.com</u>

This book is intended to be a FREE Resource for future scholarship recipients.

Others may order copies of this book
"From Whence We Came – College Survival Toolkit"
Send $12 check or money order to
LEAP Forward, Inc.
P.O. Box 373
Prince Frederick, MD 20678
Payable to "LEAP Forward, Inc."
CashApp: leap4ward

NOTES FOR MY JOURNEY

_____

_____

_____

_____

_____

_____

_____

_____

_____

_____

_____

_____

_____

_____

_____

_____

_____

_____

NOTES FOR MY JOURNEY

NOTES FOR MY JOURNEY

NOTES FOR MY JOURNEY